Pressing
RESET
—— for the ——
High School
Athlete

original
strength

Pressing RESET for the High School Athlete

Published by OS Press, Fuquay-Varina, NC

Contributor: Suzie Gullett Bachelor's Motor Learning and Development - Original Strength Certified PRO - ACE Personal Trainer - cert FMT - certificate level 3 MELT instructor - BASI Comprehensive Cert instructor- Strength Matters kettlebell instructor

ISBN: 978-1-963675-05-4 (Paperback)

Pressing RESET for the High School Athlete

Every year, a new crop of athletes enters High school, seeking to better themselves and continue their dream of playing sports at the next level. While many of these athletes practice their given sport for hours a week or year-round, they are missing one essential link to their athletic success: the ability to control injury and feel resilient after each workout or game.

Pressing RESET for the High School Athlete is here to help connect the player with his or her best movement on and off the field.

Three groups of people who will learn from *Pressing RESET for the High School Athlete* include:

- The parents will learn there are simple, repeatable steps to help their athlete recover better.

- The coach who wants to have a better handle on movement and getting their athlete back on the field and, in the words of Dan John, Strength Coach, "Are you good to go?"

- And, of course, the athlete who wants to feel better and start building a few tools in his or her toolkit to help them feel, recover, and move better, on and off the court or field of play.

Preparing for any sport takes time and many days, which can be a grind. It doesn't have to be that way. Movement prep can feel good, and you can learn to move better without more pain. Using Original Strength's Pressing RESET method starts with the desire to move pain-free and help your body progress as it is ready. Pressing RESET for the High School Athlete is about moving within your body's natural design, allowing you to accomplish more than you may have imagined. Every athlete wants to play at the highest level they can.

We will break down the three pillars of human movement:

- Proper Breathing
- Eye and head control
- Gate or contra-lateral patterns

You will learn simple, repeatable solutions for stiff, sore, tight hips, ankles, knees, and shoulders. These movements we refer to as RESETS. We start by resetting your nervous system to handle the physical demands of your sport better and move better throughout your life. By learning each RESET, you will learn to connect your upper and lower body and the right and left sides of your body.

Don't worry—there aren't secret exercises or particular patterns you must learn or adhere to. There is no secret to Pressing RESET; you can mix up the movements and have fun doing them. The key is to remember the three pillars of movement. Pressing RESET starts with breathing the way you were designed to breathe. From there, you will learn to let your eyes lead your head, and finally, you'll work to connect your brain to the rest of your body better. We will move within your natural design and then add performance and skill-based movements.

We are not teaching and coaching the right and wrong ways to move. We are trying to maximize your unique body's design to help you be your best self.

This booklet will guide you through some movements to help you restore your original strength.

High school athletes spend 4-6 hours a day just sitting. Sitting can diminish many natural movements, from breathing issues to balance problems to stiff, sore, and tired muscles susceptible to injury.

A note about sitting

Sitting for an extended period can lead to compensations in movement. Sitting can shorten the quadriceps, rotate the pelvis, put stress on the SI joints, and diminish the reflective nature of the glutes. Sitting for extended periods, as most high school athletes do, must be addressed. Pressing RESET for the High School Athlete helps address body function. It can help restore the reflexive movements of the body so the athlete can transition better from the classroom to the field of competition.

Special Note: Movement and Exercise have risks associated with them. Research shows they can lead to being stronger, healthier, and happier. However, they can also lead to injuries or even death. It happens. You should also know that doing nothing also has risks associated with it. Research shows that being sedentary can lead to sickness, weakness, frailty, depression, and anxiety. It can also make you more injury-prone and hasten your destination towards death. It happens.

Before beginning any exercise program, consult your trusted family physician. You should also consult your trusted family physician before engaging in any sedentary lifestyle.

"Every man dies, but not every man really lives."
- William Wallace, Braveheart

Pillars of Movement

*He set the earth on its foundations;
it can never be moved.*
– Psalm 104:5 NIV

Athletes may move in great and awe-inspiring ways. Some seem to defy gravity. Some break records and others just seem full of grace and effortlessness. How did they get that way? Are most athletes born with some magical superpower?

No! All athletes, including everyday athletes, are built on the three Pillars of Movement. The stronger and more resilient these pillars are, the better the athlete.

Once again, those pillars are:

- Breathing diaphragmatically.
- Moving our eyes and our heads (activating our vestibular system).
- Use contralateral patterns & crossing our mid-line (crawling, walking, cross-crawl).

These are the Pillars of Human Movement. If you build your body on these pillars, you will unleash your true design.

We must breathe. Since we spend our whole lives breathing, we should do it using our design to do it. Our mouth wasn't designed as our primary breathing vessel, and breathing through your mouth can diminish the quality of your breathing in your sport.

Our eyes and head must work together to balance our body for movement—even movements we aren't quite aware of all the time. Eye and head movements are controlled by and connected to our vestibular system, the system within the nervous system that controls the righting of our body, otherwise known as our balance.

As athletes, we must use contralateral patterns. Imagine your body as an X (put your hands up and out a bit and your feet about shoulder-width apart). Your belly button is the center of the X. Contralateral patterns are when one side of your X crosses over to the opposite side or your right hand moves forward as your left leg moves forward. The movement patterns shown here can be broken down and simplified or advanced to become more refined for the specific demands of any sport.

We rely on these pillars in everyday movement and athletic development. So, even if you aren't on the team of your dreams, you can move better by ensuring your pillars are solid.

By learning to develop your pillars of movement first, you will create a mindset of awareness. Again, the more solid your pillars, the better you'll move, react, and recover. Throughout the rest of this book, we will focus on Pressing RESET on the systems that strengthen these pillars.

What is a Baseline?

Start by checking how you move, a system status check of sorts. In sports, there are many tests to test your readiness for that sport. A famous test is the NFL Combine. It tests speed, agility, vertical strength, and body composition. This **...Good, Better, Best...** test, and tests like this for other sports, help set a baseline for movement and predict how that athlete will or could perform if selected in the draft.

We also test when Pressing RESET. We test to see where our body starts in movement so you can see how the body responds to movement. Your body is good. You aren't broken. Even if you are dealing with an injury, you still have the capacity for some movement.

Wherever you start is "your good," and it is "your baseline." You will then move to better and then to best. A wise person once said, "It feels good to feel good." We negate good feelings because we fear feeling bad. Pain or that feeling is just the body's request for change. You may need to adjust your position, the time, or the intensity of your movement, but that doesn't mean you should stop moving.

Let's start by determining your baseline, a simple, repeatable movement where we avoid moving into pain. Any movement can be a baseline. This could be a toe touch (forward fold), squat, push-up, etc. Use these baselines to help you know what your body does or to check in with your movement if you feel you are losing intensity or control of movement.

Determine Your Baseline

Choose one baseline movement (Forward fold or Squat).

Perform the movement slowly.

Remember—do not move into pain. Pain is your brain (nervous system) telling you to stop, which is different from the feeling of a stretch or stiffness.

Consider:
How do you feel?
Is there tension?
How low can you go?

How do your hamstrings, knees, calves, back, shoulders, and neck feel when you lower and come back up?
Do your knees bend when you touch your toes, or do your knees cave in while you squat?

Ask a friend, teammate, or coach to take a picture of you or examine your movement for reference.

Remember, you are not looking for "perfect"; you are just seeing what you see, feeling what you feel.

If you get used to doing a baseline check before and after each workout or even on game day, you can better understand how your body is feeling. Using the baseline check will help you learn to be aware of movements that might prevent you from performing your best and recovering your best.

You are just seeing what you see, feeling what you feel.

Note on baseline checks.

If you choose a movement you always feel your best at, you may not see or feel the changes your body is making. We will see more noticeable results when we try something more challenging. Minor changes can also be quite profound. However, seeing the larger changes in sports and athletic movements is helpful. So if you can do a "perfect" squat or you know you can easily and readily put your hands on the floor during a forward fold, switch out your baseline movement for another one, or if you want further help, Go to Originalstrength.net/videos and look up baseline movements.

Now that you have established your baseline, it's time to compare it to the 3 Pillars of Movement.

The Big Five RESETS

For a reset to be a RESET, it must include at least one of the Pillars. Some RESETS are going to feel better than others. Some will help you move better, and others may cause you not to move as well. You aim to see which ones work best and feel best for your body. Your best friend may see excellent results with one that does not work well for you. It's OK! Your body is not their body. Our focus is maximizing **your** nervous system connections, which make your whole body more responsive and resilient.

Let's practice our Good, Better, Best awareness.

Pressing
RESET

Breathing

(SPECIFICALLY NASAL & DIAPHRAGMATIC) BREATHING

As a modern culture, many have defaulted to a by-mouth approach to breathing during exercise, falsely assuming that we cannot adequately oxygenate ourselves by breathing through our noses. George Dallam, Ph.D. Professor, National Teams Coach for USA Triathlon

Lay on the floor (note: you can do all these movements in any position. Lying down, sitting, or standing)

When we lay down, we often feel more at ease. However, if lying down while actively participating in your sport isn't an option, standing is a great way to practice this and all the other RESETS as well.

Baseline

Nasal breathing Reset

Recheck Baseline

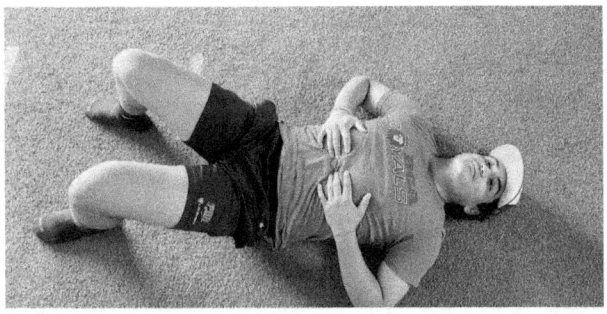

Whichever posture you choose or can do, keep your
eyes open, mouth closed, and tongue on the roof of your
mouth

- Lay on the floor, comfortably on your back and arms by
  your side with your palms up. If you have pain in your
  lower back, you may bend your knees.

- Placing your tongue on the roof of your mouth with your mouth closed (swallow and your tongue should rise to the roof of your mouth)

- Begin to breathe through your nose(keeping your mouth closed), feeling your ribs expand and a slight rise in your belly. Notice if your shoulders are rising or if you are breathing into your chest. If so, slow your inhale and let the breath exhale with less or no force.

- Continue to breathe through your nose for about 1 minute, or if you don't have a clock or someone to help you, take about 10 to 15 breaths.

After you finish your minute
Stand up
Recheck your baseline(forward fold or squat)

Baseline Re-check

Ask yourself or have your coach or teammate give you feedback. Are you,

"Good" (the same as you were at the start)

"Better" (moved with more ease or was able to go lower or a little deeper)

"Best" (best I have felt. Able to move past any area I was previously stuck)

Breathing diaphragmatically is key to your performance. It will allow you to perform better and longer. It will help you sleep better, grow your muscles and allow you to think more clearly. It will also improve your blood flow and how your body creates and transmits your hormones. Mouth closed, tongue on top of mouth behind your front teeth, will change your life.

Whatever you or your coach or teammate were able to notice was excellent and a great start! You may have your first "Ah-ha" moment. If so, you have seen that your body RESETS itself to its more natural design just by breathing. Ready to go further? Let's go!

RESET #2

Eye and Head movements

(connecting you to your vestibular system)

In sports, your eyes are critical. Often, you are running in one direction and looking in another. But where your eyes won't go is even more crucial. Watching your eyes move without standing in front of a mirror is tough. If your eyes don't want to go somewhere (up or down or right and left), your brain often stops your movement before you start.

Note: You will either set a timer for 1 minute or do 10 to 15 repetitions of each of these following movements.

- Lay back on the floor.

Let's see how your head and eyes may be affecting your movement.

Eye movements: Up and down

- Begin by doing your Nasal breathing again.
- Then, begin to move your eyes up and down. Yep, just your eyes.
- Look toward your eyebrows, then look toward your chin.
- Keep repeating this for 1 min or 10-15 repetitions
- Stand back up
- Recheck your baseline

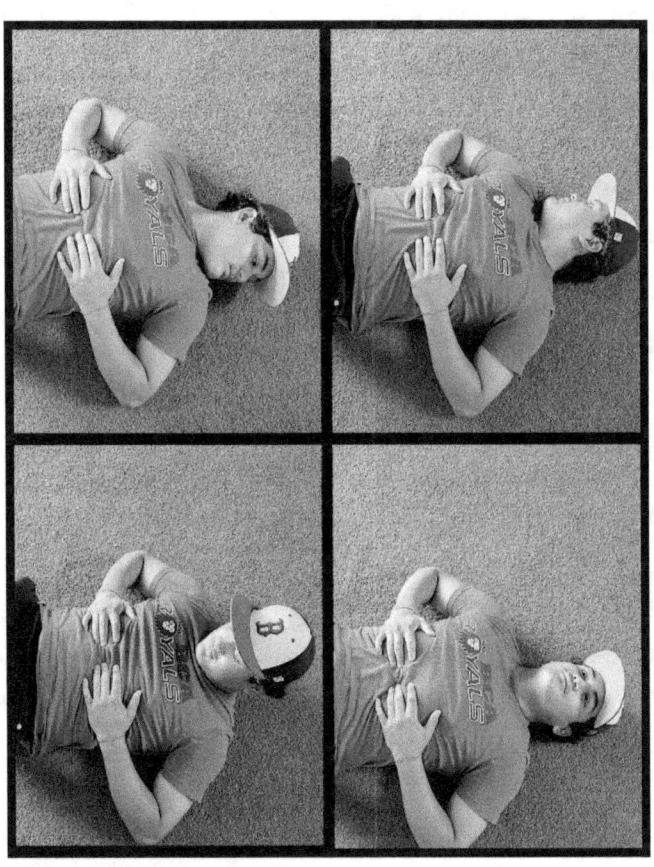

So? Good, Better, or Best?

A "little better" Okay Great!! Let me ask you this? "Have you ever done something on land at 300 miles per hour"? Well, maybe not physically, but your nervous system has, on the inside. Your nervous system moves at about 300 miles per hour.

So, that "little better" you just experienced is your nervous system saying I feel safe, so I'm giving you more freedom. Faster than a blink, your nervous system has changed. Even a "little better" is better.

If you can recover or change your movement at the speed of your nervous system at rest, you can change your system while playing your sport.

Let's see if we can get even closer to better.

Repeat the same sequence, but move your eyes right and then left (side to side) instead of up and down.

Note: While eye tracking up and down indicates a possible restriction in movement forward and back, side-to-side movement of the eyes helps identify any restriction with rotation on the left or right side of your body. Where your eyes go, your head and body will follow. If your eye movements are cautious, your head and body will follow the eye's lead.

Eye movements from side to side.

- Lie down on your back.
- Begin by doing your Nasal breathing again.
- Then, slowly begin to move your eyes from side to side. Yep, just your eyes.
- Look toward your right ear and then look toward your left ear.
- Try not to move your head yet.
- Repeat for 1 minute or 10-15 repetitions
- Stand up
- Recheck your baseline

So? Good, Better, or Best?

Let's keep going. Good things are just beginning.

Now add the head movements.

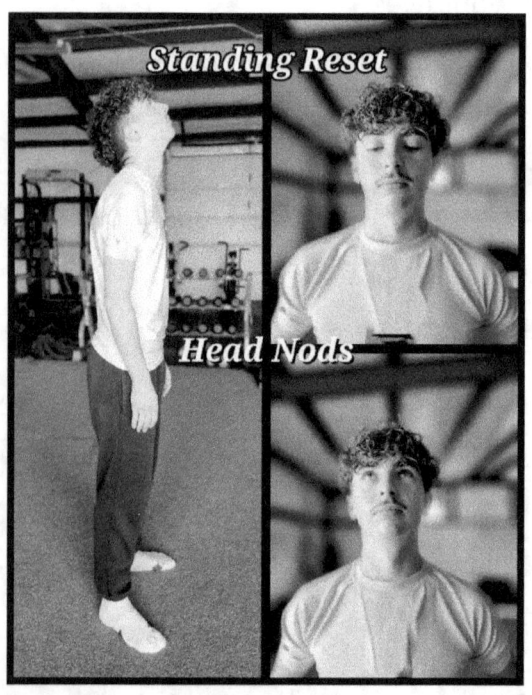

Lay on the ground. Begin with your nasal breathing, move your eyes up and then down, and tip your head up and down (like motioning "yes").

Repeat the breathing with the eye and head movements for 1 minute or 10-15 repetitions.

Recheck baseline

Do the same with side-to-side eye movement and head turns (like motioning "No.")

Recheck your baseline.

So? Good, Better, or Best?

When your coach says, "Get your head in the game" or "lock-in," you have a tool to do this.

You can do this on the field or the bench while waiting to sub in. Give yourself every opportunity to connect with your best movement. Your body was designed to move well and at a high competition level. When you give yourself a way to check in and then make a simple change of breath or RESET your ability to allow your nervous system to assist you and not overprotect you, **you will** move better, play better, and recover better.

RESET #3

Rolling

Rolling is a precursor to our walking pattern. Most athletes' movements, if captured in slow motion or a still shot, will look like an upper-body segmental or lower-body segmental roll.

Whether serving in volleyball, pitching in baseball, or lining up a corner kick in soccer, our body is in a segmental rolling position. Rolling connects the upper and lower body and can help to find areas that may feel stuck or at ease. When we connect the breath, eye, and head RESETS to rolling, great things can happen.

Rolling can be done lying on your back or belly and start from the upper or lower body. An athlete can allow, for instance, the upper body to rest after a long practice or game by initiating movement from the lower body, allowing the body to rest, and allowing the RESETS to continuously enhance the body's Good, Better, and BEST movement.

Add rolling to support your movement before or after your sports-based practice or within a series of RESETS. Segmental rolling is shown in both the Upper and Lower body RESETS later in the book.

RESET #4

Rocking

Now that you have seen and experienced what breathing and eye and head control can do, let's see how the body responds when we give it a simple reminder to reset to another fundamental movement pattern.

The squat is a movement pattern that most people think of when they go to the weight room. It is the precursor to jumping and sprinting. Squatting started when we were little kids. We would play sitting in a squat. Now, as a High School athlete, you use the squat all the time and in nearly all sports.

The Squat starts on the ground in a horizontal position, moves to an upright position as you get stronger, and then to a power position.

We tie the body together by adding other body motions to our breathing and eye and head control movements. In other words, we are starting to take all the parts and make them whole. With all that, we can make skill look effortless and strength, power, and speed, feel invincible.

- Get down on the floor/ground.
- Start on all fours (hands and knees). With your tongue on the roof and your mouth closed, keep your head in line with your back, and your eyes on the horizon begin to rock back and forth.
- Curl your toes under
- Rock backward so your hips move toward your heels and then forward so your shoulders move over your wrists (notice that when you rock back toward your feet, this looks like a squat position).

Note: The rocking positions can be done on all fours, in a half-kneeling position, in a kickstand position

where one leg is extended out away from the body, in all ranges of motion, and with many different hand positions. They are also subtle core moves that can calm the nervous system.

Repeat this rocking for about 1 minute(or more) or 10-20 repetitions.

Recheck your Baseline

So, Good, Better, or Best?

Frequently, whether you chose the forward fold or the squat, at this point, both movements have moved from your baseline from Good to better or maybe even BEST.

We showed you that the body can change at the speed of the nervous system, which can move at 300 miles an hour. Pressing RESET on the nervous system allows these changes. It can take you from feeling sore, stuck, and tired to a personal best, higher rebounds, a faster 40, or simply simply feeling

better. Remember, it feels good to feel good.

Contralateral Patterns

Whether your goal is upper body, core, or even cardiovascular strength, crawling can support all of these goals. The crawling RESET comes from the rocking RESET and connects us through contralateral movements. Crawling can be done on your front, side, or back. Each way you travel can help you or your athlete RESET and strengthen their hips, shoulders, and posture. Crawling is designed to be done from the ground up, just like we learn to walk: the baby-crawl on hands and knees, the leopard-crawl with knees off the ground, or a cross-crawl from a standing position. Each position of this RESET can develop balance and control across the X of the body and help to support the other RESETS. Add crawling to any upper or lower body RESET as a strength component.

Set a timer for 1-3 minutes ⏲

With tongue on the roof of mouth and mouth closed, breathing through your nose.

Start with the forward baby crawling 3-4 feet, then crawl backward, and then crawl sideways.

Your hips, shoulders, and core learn to become better and then their best.

This can be done with your knees on the ground (baby-crawl) or with your knees off the ground (leopard-crawl)

Stretching vs. Moving

When did you last see a 5-year-old stretch before playing? How about a dog about to chase a squirrel? Remember, your brain's primary job is to keep you safe. Suppose you feel the need to stretch to perform. In that case, you are likely overriding your body's safety system designed to protect you from injury. Press RESET rather than stretching.

Stretching tends to be muscle-focused, while Pressing RESET is movement-focused. Usually, stretching focuses on one muscle at a time. Pressing RESET allows the body's natural tendency to tie itself together in its natural design.

Pressing RESET is a movement-focused approach that aligns with your body's natural design. It empowers your nervous system to optimize movement, improving performance and preventing injury. You can unlock your full athletic potential by prioritizing RESETS and trusting your body's innate wisdom. Your body is designed to move well before, during, and after any sport or event you might play—even in everyday life.

An Every Day Reset for High School Athletes.

As an athlete or coach, or maybe you are an everyday athlete who wants to move better, we must look at ourselves with more than just movement in mind. How do we move, why do we move, for what purpose do we move, and can I move better tomorrow? Realize it takes an athlete years to shave 1 second off their time in a race. It takes years to develop the movements to dance a ballet.

Most sports are about the time you put into your diet, strength and conditioning, skill development, and mindset. So, achieving any outstanding lasting result takes more than three minutes. However, the body can still change at the speed of the nervous system, so what if you decide every day to treat your nervous system like your own personal trainer? What if you do a movement where your body tells you how it is working, and you see cause and effect in as little as 10 minutes a day? The Pressing RESET method can help you move and free up extra time to play better.

As you move forward, remember there is NO SPECIAL FORMULA for Pressing RESET. The sequences given are to give you a place to begin. As you become better at seeing what your body sees, you can refine and rework any of these sequences laid out for you. Remember, some things work for one person, and not everything works for everyone. Discover, play, learn, listen, and become a world-class mover. Your body is designed to move and to move well your entire life. Yes, that includes high-level athletics and everyday opportunities. Be curious.

When to move is not the problem. Learning to move and allowing yourself to become great at movement on or off the field is what to focus on. Take opportunities to move after or before every game, or meet or match. If you spent 10 minutes RESETTING your movement and learning and allowing that supercharged nervous system to work for you, think about how well you could move during your event and how much quicker you would recover.

Try this daily RESET

Before you begin, think about this. When you move through the RESETS, these are just movement-based patterns. Any basic human movement can be a RESET in itself. Somebody may use a push-up to develop upper body strength and be a RESET movement. It's the intention of the movement. Intention is the secret sauce to reaching your goals. What is your intention for this movement? Exercise or RESET or both? Or, just maybe, to feel good.

Set a timer for 10 minutes 🕐

If you can, have the timer beep every minute. If you don't have an interval timer, set a timer for ten minutes and do each of these RESETS for 10 to 20 repetitions. If you have a dominant arm or leg in your sport, it's okay if the nondominant arm or leg does more reps than the other.

Begin with a baseline movement (forward fold, squat, or the lowering phase of a push-up)

Start your timer/clock 🕐

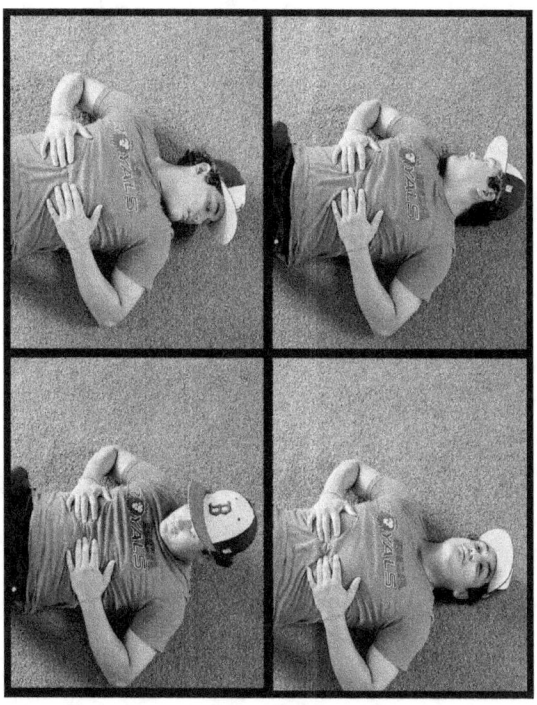

1:00 Nasal Breathing: Lay on the floor on your back with your palms up by your side and begin to breathe with your mouth closed and tongue against the roof of your mouth.

2:00 Eyes and head nods: Begin to look toward your eyebrows and then to your chin. When you feel comfortable, add your head nod, chin to chest, and lift your head to look toward your knees.

3:00 Eyes and Head turns: Begin to look with your eyes left and right. When you feel ready, turn your head, letting your eyes lead your head.

Windshield Wiper

Knees side to side

Dead bug

4:00   Windshield wipers: Slide your knees toward your hips until your feet are flat on the floor about hip distance apart. Let your knees lower to the left and right like windshield wipers. Keep your shoulders on the ground.

5:00   Knees side to side: Bring your knees to your chest, and then, twisting your core, lower your knees left and right. Stop short of them touching the ground on either side. Think 10 and 2 like on a clock.

6:00   Dead Bug: Bring arms in line with the knees, not letting the elbow bend. Take your right arm over your head as you extend your left leg. Bring both arm and leg back to the start, and repeat on the other side with the left arm and right leg.

7:00:   Lower body segmental Roll: Lower the legs back to the floor and take your arms over your head so your Body is the shape of an X. Bend your right knee and bring it to your chest, and roll your right knee to the left side of your body and kick out and back in, then roll back to the starting position. Do the same roll starting from the left side, bringing your left knee into your chest

8:00:   Upper body segmental roll: Arms are overhead in the X. Begin by looking to the right side of the body with your eyes, then lift your head in that direction. Lift your left arm and reach toward "9 o'clock" while continuing to look to the right and roll back into place. Repeat with the right arm; eyes look, head lifts, and arm follows, reaching toward "3 o'clock".

9:00: Lay on the floor like you started, on your back, arms by your side. Return to your nasal breathing for the last minute.

When the timer goes off, stand up and recheck your baseline.

So, Good, Better, or Best?

You can practice this as much as you'd like each day or keep to a schedule and do it in the morning or before bed.

Check out our website to see a video of this Everyday RESET.

https://www.youtube.com/@OriginalStrengthSystem

The sum of all movements depends on one thing: Breathing

We could mention every sport here with specific and detailed movement RESETS. But there are common areas that you can focus on to keep you moving and feeling great. Whether before or after, or indeed during each game. Remember the power of your breath. Your breath controls every function of your body. Respiration isn't just inhaling and exhaling from the outside; each muscle, organ, and cell has respiration. So, suppose you can first always pay attention to your breathing. In that case, it is foundational to calming you down, releasing your stress, and clearing your way to a better mindset. You will control one of the most powerful recovery and readiness tools anyone can utilize.

"When the race gets hard, I know it's imperative that I keep my form...keeping my breathing steady and relaxed helps me stay focused and allows me to stay loose and maintain my focus, make every movement move better."
- Mo Farrah, 7x Olympic Gold medalist

Upper body Feels stuck Throwing/Hitting/Sprinting

Sports often fall into categories of upper-body or lower-body dominance. Legs and/or arms are used and overused for jumping, landing, changing direction, and even stopping.

Some sports are full-body—swimming, gymnastics, and martial arts. But whether your sport is upper, lower, dominant, or full body, or if you are using a dominant arm or leg in the performance of that sport, you must use your eyes and head, and for sure, you must breathe. Your eye and head movements help to control where your body is about to go, and your breathing is by design, allowing you to

You are trying to help your body find its best movement.

relax or intensify your movements. By linking the body and breath together, your movements can be more powerful, but you can also control the stress of the movements.

In some sports, your throwing needs to be exact. Hitting requires balanced eye and hand coordination. Even when sprinting, you must keep your head up. Your arms move at an intense pace, even for a relatively short time. The RESETS help when the upper body gets stuck, sore, and tired. They can help unlock, allowing you to move at your best and feel your best even after a long game or practice.

Remember, there are many movements within movements when resetting your body. Where you put your hands, how you hold your head, or if you are breathing with your mouth open can change the outcome of each RESET. So be patient with yourself. You aren't just trying to do these RESETS right; you are trying to help your body find its best movement. So, this will be difficult to understand in the world of specific times, rankings, and results. But the best movers move with a sense of play or curiosity. Don't get too stuck on the "right" way to do each RESET. Let your body teach you how it wants to move and when it is ready to move.

Pressing RESET for upper body

Do a baseline movement.

Set a timer for 10 minutes ⏱

1. Lay on your stomach and place your head in your hands like a pillow

    »   Start with nasal breathing, then come up to your forearms for eye and head movements.

    »   Push yourself back to a semi-all-fours with your forearms still on the ground.

2. Commando Rocking: Begin rocking back and forth, bringing your hips toward your heels and shoulders toward your hands. Feel the movement under your arms, even behind your armpits, into your ribs as you rock forward and back.

Commando Rocking

3. Knees rocking

4. Knees rocking circles

5. Single arms, knees rocking

6. Bird Dogs

7. Skiers

8. Thoracic rotation

9. Quarter segmental rolls from belly Upper body

10. Return to your breathing for the last minute

https://originalstrength.net/book-videos/upper-body/

For a sample video, use this QR code.

Lower body Tight and Achy Jumping/Running/Change of Direction

As with the RESETS for the upper body, the lower body gets a lot of work in any sport. Regarding lower-body work, you will also be helping balance and power for every movement of your sport.

In every sport, the lower body takes a beating: in baseball, your hips; in track, your hamstrings; in volleyball, your knees; and in basketball, your ankles. Every sport has dominant areas prone to movement imbalances, strains, sprains, stiffness, soreness, and tightness after a game or even before.

Your legs will take you to the next level of your sport. But they can also hold you back if they are constantly stiff, sore, and tired. When our legs aren't moving their best, our body makes up for all the power and explosiveness required from some other muscle or structure that is no longer doing its primary function.

Remember, your body is designed to move. Since your body is like an X, what you do to the lower half will affect the upper half, which is helpful, especially if you feel short on time or space.

Athletes move in all directions, and you need to be able to feel how your body responds to movement so you can make small adjustments on and off the field.

In this next RESET example, you can make small changes to the feet or hand position to help change the focus of the RESET.

Lower Body RESET

Check your baseline

Set a timer for 12 minutes. At the top of each minute, switch to the next RESET. It is not essential to stay in an exact rep range as it is to begin learning to listen to how your body feels (good, better, or best) in or during each RESET.

Allow yourself to get comfortable with the movements, and then allow time to help you move better.

The following is an example of moving through this Lower Body RESET. No RESET has hard and fast rules or time that you must adhere to to get the best results. As each athlete practices the RESET, they will come to understand which RESET helps them feel Good, Better, or their Best. Use these RESETS as a guideline.

Use the time "In-Between" Races, periods, halftime, or when you may feel off and want to get locked in.

Start laying on your stomach

Press start on your timer (12 minutes)

:00 Begin to breathe, mouth closed, through your nose

1:00

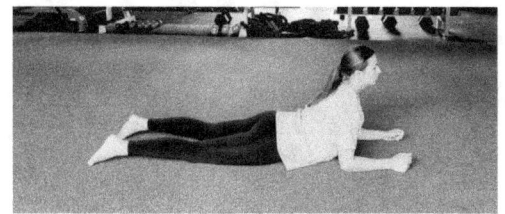

2:00

 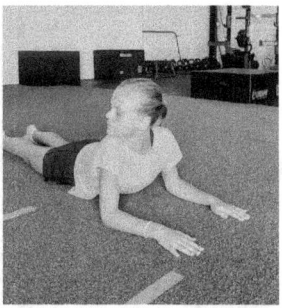

3:00

4:00

5:00

6:00

7:00

8:00

9:00

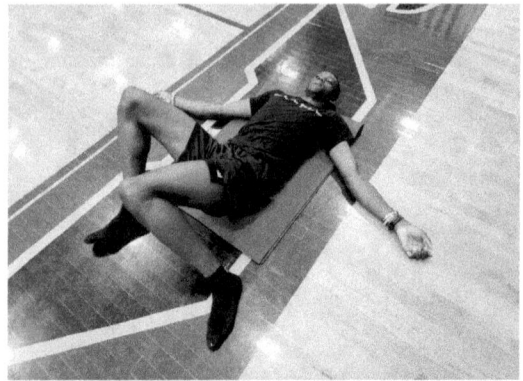

10:00

11:00

https://originalstrength.net/book-videos/lower-body/
{QR CODE}

For a sample video, use this QR code.

The In-between

"If it's important, then do it every day."
– Dan John

The in-between is where the magic really happens, and you differentiate yourself from the other players who come to play but not to win and then win again the next day. Athleticism isn't just about doing your sport but doing all it takes to be the best, thinking of what the other guy or gal isn't doing, and doing that even more.

You don't play every minute of every game. There are 10, 20, or even 30 minutes between games or halves when you could spend even 3 minutes Pressing RESET. Even giving yourself what seems a short time to focus is the focus someone else is not putting in and will provide you with the edge.

You can learn to throw the ball, make a goal, or even increase your vertical height for a spike. You have learned, trained, and developed these skills. Your design goes with you wherever you are—no matter what inning, quarter, or race. Do you want more from each skill you have worked hours on and spent hundreds, if not thousands, of dollars on to develop? **Do the in-between!** Reset your breathing, eye, head, and contralateral movement patterns. It may only take 1 minute.

Athletic RESETS Anytime, Anywhere

"I can't predict what the future brings. I can only focus my attention and energy on the present moment and do what I do best, and that is to try to prepare myself."
– Novak Djokovic, tennis player.

Standing Reset

3 minutes ⏱

The 3 Pillars

Breathing

- Start standing feet level, eyes looking out at the horizon
- Resting hands on your belly or around your ribs so you can feel your breath
- Breath through your mouth, close your tongue on the roof of your mouth for 1 minute

Eye and head movements

- Begin looking up with eyes followed by the head. Chin comes to chest, eyes look up, and back of the head touches shoulders 1 minute (30 seconds each)

- Look to the right and left with your eyes leading your head like you are saying "no."

Contralateral movements

- Rotate your arms around your torso, letting your arms hit your sides.
- Remember to breathe with your mouth closed.
  - » Let your eyes lead your head, and your head lead your body. Move all the way to your feet.
  - » Make sure your hips and heels rotate as well. 1 minute

It takes less time, and you don't have to do a wide variety. The body likes to repeat movements until it is very confident with them. Think of walking. Even though walking doesn't seem very athletic, walking is truly the foundation of all athletic movements and a perfect RESET. Walking includes balance, proprioception, contralateral movement, speed, and control. Walking tells us where our body is in space and connects us to our breathing and eye and head movements. It's a RESET within a RESET and can help to tie the body together.

If you feel sore, stuck, tired, or having difficulty focusing or keeping your mind right, go for a walk. It doesn't have to be long. Even walking for as little as 10 minutes can change your outlook and help you to feel better and move better. Just remember to connect all the pillars of movement. Keep your tongue on the roof of your mouth, breathing through your nose, and allow your eyes and head to look around while you Press RESET while walking.

Like walking, there are other RESETS that you can do by yourself, which help tie the X together, calm the mind, and develop strength and stability.

The Skier

You have already done this RESET when Pressing RESET for the whole body. The beautiful "aha" moment with the skier often is how much better your overhead extension gets and how you can feel your shoulders connect with your hips.

You will not only find that this is simple, but it may profoundly affect your baseline. We often confuse simple with unnecessary or unnecessary for those more advanced in movement. Simple is just that simple. Simple helps movements become repeatable and simplifies more complex movements you perform in your given sport.

To do this simple RESET, set yourself up on all fours (quadruped position),

Set a timer for 1-3 minutes or up to 10 minutes.

- Start in a quadruped position
- begin to reach your right arm back toward your right hips
- At the same time, extend your left leg straight back.

(Make a "swish" sound like you were skiing down a mountain)

- Repeat on the left side
- Continue to do the skier - right arm and left leg back and left Arm to hips/ right leg back toward wall
  » Keep your chest up or a proud chest
  » Mouth closed tongue on the roof of the mouth

Rocking

The "ready position" is a position that almost every sport uses. The ready position is a squat where the athlete is on their toes, with the arms typically held in front of the eyes and head up, ready to receive the ball or play. Rocking is the RESET that best matches this movement.

You can do variations of rocking, with both knees on the floor and one knee on the floor, called half kneeling. It can even be done off the knees, hands on a chair or wall, or knees off the floor.

Single-arm, half-kneeling, commando, Kickstand, and more are just some of the many rocking positions. Each position can support the body's natural and even more specific movements for a given sport. Remember, our original design is to move well.
Try different variations and see how each might impact your movement: "Good," "Better," or "Best."

If you are having difficulty with your squat or your knees or feet just aren't feeling right, try these alternate foot position RESETS of Knees rocking

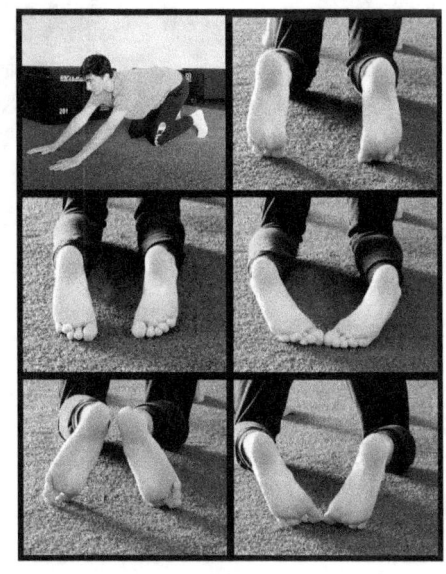

Prepping for baseball or loosening hips

1/2 kneeling

Kickstand

Knees rocking variations

Wide leg

Tight Shoulders?

Commando Rocking

An excerpt from *Original Strength Performance: The Next Level (Anderson, Morton, Shropshire)*

"When all the joints move together freely but in unison, the brain feels safe enough to remove any limitations it may have placed on the body. Limitations like pain, stiffness, and weakness often melt away when the brain knows where everything in the body is. Rocking lets the brain know where everything is!

Another wonderful benefit to rocking is that, along with uniting the whole body in a beautiful physical flow, it unites the whole person, inside and out. Rocking soothes the soul. When the brain feels safe and gets all the information it seeks, the emotions and thoughts will also be peaceful and relaxed. Rocking is a fantastic way to literally move your cares away, melt tension out of your body, and stress out of your soul."

Whether rocking on one knee or two or with your knees off the floor, rocking feels great. As athletes, you often need a go-to movement to keep in your tool kit to pull out in any and every situation. Rocking really will do that for you.

Whether you only have time to rock for 1 minute or can really enjoy a 3-minute rocking RESET, put your body and mind on track during a game (of course on the sidelines) or before to help the body feel at ease.

Try Rocking now.

Check out your baseline.

Set up a timer for between 1 and 3 minutes

Now, let's try it. Remember to think of a "ready position" but just on the floor.

- Get on your hands and knees. All fours or quadruped position
- Find something to look at across the room so your head and eye can focus on something.
- Keep your chest up or a proud chest
- Mouth closed tongue on the roof of the mouth
- Gently rock back and forth by rocking your hips towards your feet, then rock your body forward over your hands.
  - » Keep your chest tall throughout, notice if your head drops, and try to keep it up, looking at that spot across the room.
- Try out different foot positions just like you would for your sport
  - » Toes pointed back
  - » Toes curled under(body position like a squat)
  - » Heels in, toes out, or toes in, heels out

Play with this. Yes, play. Your sport is a skill requiring you to repeat until it is flawless and smoothly flows from you. You are designed to play effortlessly but with curiosity, finding new ways to move each time you rock.

- Each time you Press RESET, you will learn something about yourself and your movement if you are willing.

- Every new season, you can apply more from each of the pillars of movement to your movement prep, the game, and your recovery.

- Anywhere, any time you decide to Press RESET, you will be changing and challenging the nervous system to respond from a place of ease rather than fear.

- Whatever RESET you do, do it with curiosity and play.

- It's okay to feel good. Turns out it feels good to feel good.

Now, go, practice these RESETS. You will see how amazing your design is when you do them.

If you want more information on Original Strength or any support, please contact Original Strength.

Check out our YouTube channel and bodcast to help and encourage you as you Press RESET throughout your high school years...and beyond.

https://www.youtube.com/@OriginalStrengthSystem

One more thing:

Anyone can go through these movements. You were designed to move this way.

A high school swimmer came to me when she changed seasons to begin track. Her thighs or quads were hurting even while walking. She felt like she was falling behind, and the season had just started.

At the speed of the nervous system

I took her through the baseline line assessment (OSSA) and then began with breathing. When we rechecked her assessments, she had no pain and could walk with no pain as well. She felt her best!

This athlete was now able, at the speed of the nervous system, to allow for better breathing, simple eye and head movements, and reintegrated contralateral patterns. In about five minutes, she had no more pain and felt more confident. It was as if she could go to practice because she now felt successful in her ability to move well.

Remember, you aren't fragile. You are well-designed for excellence.

About the Contributor

My Name is Suzie Gullett, and I bring over 15 years of extensive experience working with High School athletes in various settings. I have a proven track record of success in private settings, group settings, and with teams of all sorts. My work has spanned across different sports, including Swimming, Football, Soccer, Basketball, Tennis, Wrestling, Volleyball, and Track and Field. In the development of athletes, I have observed a strong emphasis on do-it-yourself strength and conditioning, with some focus on improving movement with less pain on your own time.

I've written three books under the 'Pressing Reset' series, each tailored to specific age levels. The first, 'Pressing RESET for Kids ', is designed to help children develop strong and healthy movement patterns. The second, 'Pressing RESET for Longevity ', focuses on maintaining optimal movement and health throughout life. Now, with 'Pressing RESET for the High School Athlete ', I aim to share my extensive experience in movement training to help you enhance your movement patterns, leading to improved performance, quicker recovery, and a better overall sense of well-being.

Movement has always been my passion. From a young age, I found joy in digging in the dirt and climbing trails. In high school, I competed in volleyball, track, and cheerleading, and later went on to train top D1, D2, and professional athletes. For me, movement is a ground-up process, and we were all designed to move and move well throughout our lives. Watching others move and become their best brings me joy, and I find my strength and joy in the Lord, who renews my strength daily.

Strength is a crucial component of wellness, and reaching any goal requires focus, determination, and perseverance. Movement is powerful and can empower our lives. Each day presents an opportunity to strive towards becoming an ageless athlete. I approach all aspects of fitness and wellness with curiosity. I hold a BS in Kinesiology and am certified as an Original Strength Pro, a kettlebell instructor, a Rocktape Movement Specialist, a BASI Comprehensive Pilates instructor, and a MELT Method Instructor. Additionally, I have owned and operated Bent on Fitness, a successful movement and training program, for over 15 years.

Currently, I serve as the Head of Athletic Development at Burlington Christian Academy in North Carolina, where I am dedicated to helping all individuals reach their athletic potential and develop movement skills for everyday living and performance. My role involves designing and implementing comprehensive training programs, conducting movement assessments, and providing personalized coaching to students. My family is the love of my life. I have been married for 30 years, and my kids are grown and starting their own lives.

I urge you to set your eyes upon Him, allowing yourself to be renewed each day by studying His great and wonderful word and leaning on Him, for He is your breath and your strength.

Suzie Gullett - bringyourbestfitness@gmail.com

Want to learn more?

This booklet is designed to give you a brief overview of Original Strength's Pressing RESET method.

We've crafted this booklet with a singular goal in mind: to empower you to unlock your full potential. The transformative power of the Pressing RESET method can help you feel better, move better, and achieve a level of performance you may not have thought possible. Even if you only implement a fraction of what's in this booklet, you'll notice significant changes in how your mind and body respond to various situations.

Original Strength Systems (OS) is the leader in nervous system restoration and development of reflexive strength. Our mission is to bring the hope and strength of movement to every body in the world. We provide accredited continuing education courses and books for health, fitness, and education professionals, empowering them to deliver better outcomes to their patients, clients, athletes, and students.

Based on the human developmental sequence, a series of movements that all humans naturally go through as they grow, and the human body's design, OS' Pressing RESET method teaches movements that help RESET an individual's neuromuscular system, allowing them to enjoy improved physical movement and physiological function.

If you're eager to learn more about Pressing RESET and reclaim your original strength, https://originalstrength.net is your gateway. There, you'll discover a wealth of resources, from comprehensive books to hundreds of free video tutorials (OS Movement Snax), and a complete directory of our courses and OS Certified Professionals in your vicinity. We're here to support you every step of the way.

If you're ready to enhance your movement system, we encourage you to connect with an OS Certified Professional. They can conduct an Original Strength Screen and Assessment (OSSA), a quick and simple method to identify areas for improvement. With the OSSA, the professional can guide you to the most effective starting point for your journey to restore your Original Strength through the Pressing RESET technique.

Remember, the OS team is always here for you. If you have any questions or need further guidance, please don't hesitate to reach out. We're committed to your journey towards better movement and health.

Please keep us updated on your progress. We want to know how you are doing. Progress@OriginalStrength.net.

Press RESET now and live life better and stronger because you are awesomely and wonderfully made to accomplish amazing things.

For more information:

Original Strength Systems, LLC
OriginalStrength.net

PressingRESETfor@Originalstrength.net

www.ingramcontent.com/pod-product-compliance
Lightning Source LLC
Chambersburg PA
CBHW071218120626
46546CB00006B/2613